I reminded

everything

together fo

do it again.

But more importantly, he didn't have to believe me right now. He just had to keep reminding himself that *I believed me.* I would hold that space and I would believe for both of us until he was back with me.

And I believe it for you, too. I'm not around to make you a casserole, but I hope you consider this my way of holding space for you, during your process. I want you to know what I know to be true. I don't just think it or believe it. I FUCKING KNOW IT. And one day, hopefully soon, I hope you know it, too.

This isn't about the recovery part, actually. This isn't the <u>Grief</u> zine or the <u>Getting Over It</u> zine. Those are for dealing with the

3

aftershocks of a terrible event. And totally worth reading if that is the space you are in.

This zine is about being down in the middle of the muck of it. Of being pretty damn sure that the light at the end of the tunnel is an oncoming fucking train, carrying a load of hantavirus and soylent green as it comes chugging towards you. This isn't about *letting go*. Because you can't let go of the safety bar when you are upside down on the roller coaster, right? This is about staying as sane as possible when shit is heavy. Because most crises aren't over quickly, are they? Life is messy, complicated, and a lot of really awful stuff gets dragged out over a long period of time.

So how do we get up every morning, feed ourselves and everyone who relies on us, find clean socks, and get out the door when we are living in a crisis state? How do we get through it?

Be In Your Experience

he very best thing you can do for yourself is do the work NOW. Because, after all, all that a trauma response is? <u>A failure of recovery</u>. The more work you are able to do during the *getting through it* part, the less work you will have to do in the *getting over it* part.

One of the basic things you can do is ground yourself back in your body. I go into grounding exercises in greater detail in my book *Unfuck Your Brain* (Microcosm, 2017). You can also use your Google-Fu if you want to read more on grounding and all the different types of grounding you can try, but the basic idea of grounding is to reconnect to what you experience.

It's a natural human response to want to disconnect from our pain. The instinct is to mentally escape from that experience, but that makes the pain worse in the long run because it stays stuck in our nervous system. So we have a vicious cycle of it getting worse and worse and escaping that pain more and more. And that's a bare bone form of survival. And you are far more likely to struggle with a trauma response after the crisis is over.

Being in your experience doesn't mean you have to lose your mind, though. Grounding is meant to help you stay in the moment and in your body AND find ways to manage feeling triggered by everything you are going through. There are three main categories of grounding techniques:

1) Mental Grounding—Play list or category games with yourself. Notice everything in the space around you, describe an activity in great detail, make lists of things (favorite TV shows, animals, whatever). This is a way of focusing your attention in the present without shutting down

2) Physical Grounding - Engage in physical change. Push your feet into the floor (barefoot or otherwise). Run cool water over your wrists. When you can reconnect with your physical body and everything you are experiencing, it allows you to

pass through high-stress body
response (read: nervous system on
high alert).

3) Soothing Grounding – Think about
the things you love, focus on
pictures of the people you love,
or plan yourself a warm bath
or a treat after a long day. A
mantra, favorite quote, or coping
statements can act as a way of
engaging in soothing grounding,
as well.

Connect With Others

We are not alone in our grief, in
our sadness, in our anger, in our
anxiety, in our depression, or in
our burdens. We are not alone in
feeling the way we do. There are other people
walking around out there. Maybe behind you

in line at the coffee shop, maybe spaced out in front of you when the light has already turned green. But they are carrying far more than any of us can imagine. Just like we are carrying far more than even the people closest to us know. You are not alone.

Which means you don't have to be isolated. People can and will be there if you let them. They can and will understand. And if they don't? They are NOT your fucking people. They are in their own shit. Which has nothing to do with your shit. And that's OK. But right now? They aren't your people. Keep looking for your people. Be open to them when they arrive.

An interesting thing about other people also hurting? This serves to remind you that you are not alone. This doesn't mean you shouldn't recognize and honor your feelings.

Or get all wrapped up in the idea that someone else has it worse. Or you should finish your broccoli because there are children starving in Africa. It isn't a competition. If it was, some person out there would have it so far worse than all the rest of us they would be the only person out there on the planet allowed to feel bad. And it doesn't work that way.

Perspective that others are also suffering is a good thing. Perspective that others may be suffering differently or more or whatever is also a good thing. But it's just that... PERSPECTIVE. It's a reminder that we aren't alone. One of the most fundamental struggles during the crisis is a feeling of being so disconnected from everyone else. Not only do others want to be there for you, there are other people also hurting. No, of course not in the same way. Situations are specific but pain is <u>universal</u>. Holding the truth of shared pain in the world is another way of combatting that feeling of isolation in your experience.

Self-Care

One of the trauma-informed therapy modalities that I use has self-care assignments built into it. Not as a general "just be nice with yourself" but as part of real healing work. It's real therapy homework. Because we need to stop punishing ourselves out of the things in life that give us joy. The world doesn't have to be completely grey just because the muck you are wading through is so very, very grey.

One of my board interns tried this with a client recently: They asked him to do something fun for himself, to break out of his stagnant routine with nothing to look forward to. Maybe go out to eat? Go sit in a coffee shop with a book? Catch a movie?

The client went indoor skydiving, y'all.

INDOOR SKYDIVING.

I can't even wrap my head around HOW FUCKING COOL that is. Right in the middle of everything he was dealing with, right in the middle of all he needed to do to get through his particular situation, he went to an indoor skydiving simulator and experienced something like freefall. Tried something he had always wanted to do, something that thrilled him, challenged him, scared him a wee bit. And it shifted his entire perspective. We were blown away.

Self-care can be as small as a dollar store bottle of nail polish and painted toenails. Or it can be as big as indoor skydiving. Or as big as you need or want it to be. But you deserve self-care NOW, not just when it's all over. A bubble bath. A soft, comfortable pair of PJ pants. One amazing cookie from a wonderful bakery. Skydiving, a road trip, a new class in something you always wanted to learn. Make space for your self-care in this. Not out of selfishness but because a doctor just told you it's an integral part of your healing.

And if a doctor tells you to do something, then you totally have to do it, right?

Self-Compassion

The difference between self-compassion and self-esteem cannot be understated. Self-esteem is extrinsic, meaning that it is dependent on what's going on around us. Didn't get the grade you expected or the raise at work? Drop in self-esteem right along with it.

Self-compassion is intrinsic. Meaning you are kind and understanding to yourself *just because you have value as a human being and deserve kindness and understanding.*

This isn't letting yourself off the hook for serious dickitude behavior. And it doesn't encourage future dickitude behavior. In fact, research in self-compassion shows just the opposite to be true. If you are kinder and gentler to yourself, and forgive yourself your shortcomings, you are way MORE likely to make better decisions for yourself in the future.

Self-compassion means giving yourself the same support you would give your best friend.

Someone you care about that was hurting. You would be firm but kind, right?

"Yeah, you messed up there. This whole situation is completely fucked. But you aren't a horrible person. This is, however, a horrible situation. And you are going through a LOT right now. Beating yourself up isn't fixing anything. Time to put on your adulting pants and get back to work. We got this."

You wanna change your life in a hurry? Start practicing self-compassion. Kristen Neff and Christopher Germer have both written some of the best stuff about self compassion I've ever read. You can find tons of it on their websites for free and their books are well worth reading.

Taking Your Power Back

When life kicks us in the ass, we feel completely disempowered. And, true statement, there is so much out there that we have zero control over. It's exhausting, overhwhelming, and StressfulAF. And we forget where we do have power. It may be a tiny, little bit. But there is something there. And finding it when in the middle of a Category 5 Shitstorm can feel like an overwhelming amount of difficult.

But really fucking important.

Finding those small spaces where you still can maintain some power may be the most important thing you can do to see yourself through. Maybe the only power you have is in your reaction to everything around you. And that is still SOMETHING. Have you ever read *Man's Search For Meaning* by Victor Frankl? If not, consider adding it to your TBR. It's theoretically a book that introduces a new kind of therapy practice (logotherapy) but it's REALLY about his experiences in a Nazi concentration camp and finding meaning in the experience by holding onto his humanity in a situation designed to strip him of it. He writes about the forced marches, and how another prisoner on one of these marches found six berries out in the woods. He picked the berries, and although starving himself, carried them back to the camp, hiding them from the guards the entire way, to bring them to a friend.

That's real power, that right there. The power to connect to other people and care for them while living through the worst thing that human beings do to other human beings.

What are your six berries? Where do you have power in this situation? What actions can you take to own this power? What would that do for you and for the situation? What's the first thing you can do when you set this down and get back to real life?

Cover art by Nate Powell

SeeMyBrotherDance.org/